RISE FIGHT LOVE REPEAT

Ignite Your Morning Fire

JEFF WICKERSHAM

RISE, FIGHT, LOVE, REPEAT

Edited by: Lori Lynn Enterprises

Cover Design by: Rodjie Ulanday

Dear Mom,

This book is dedicated to you and your legacy.

I remember that drive we took to the University of Pennsylvania for a radiation treatment in the fall of 2014. We had one of the deepest discussions we ever shared.

I remember hearing you talk about how scared you were that your grandchildren would not remember you ... that you would be forgotten ... that as the years passed, they would forget how much you loved them and cared for them.

I think, at a deeper level, you wanted to know that your life had meaning. I told you, without a doubt, that your legacy of hope and positivity would live on for generations to come.

I made a promise to you that day. A promise that I wasn't even aware of at the time. The promise to carry on your legacy. To let it live through me, my sons, and their children. This book is part of the fulfillment of that promise.

I didn't know then how the dots would connect, but looking back now, I am blown away by how they have connected.

Mom, thank you for all your love and support.

Love your son,

Jeff

CONTENTS

"Of all the forces that make for a better world, none is so powerful as hope; with hope, one can think, one can work, one can dream. If you have hope, you have everything."

—ADAPTED FROM CHARLES SAWYER

CHAPTER ONE

Your Internal Hero's Journey

What I'm going to share with you in this book isn't taught in schools. Not in elementary school, middle school, high school, or even in college. Parents don't pass it down to their children because their parents didn't pass it down to them either. It's a simple, straightforward process to unlocking your true potential. It's a blueprint for more energy, focus, abundance, and time in your life that you never thought would be possible.

Have you ever searched for that one thing? That one thing that would create the ultimate life that you have forever wanted to lead? The one thing that all highly successful people seem to have but you feel is beyond your reach? For me, personally, it was a relentless pursuit that always left me feeling empty.

That chase led me to a lot of pain and failure. I ended up where I always was, on the never-ending treadmill of life. Running as fast as I could but never getting anywhere. Does that sound familiar?

Each day seemed like *Groundhog Day*. Year after year, I was in the same place I was before. Remember that scene from the movie where Bill Murray wakes up to his alarm clock playing the same song, over and over, day after day? It was a never-ending loop from which I couldn't seem to break free.

Frustrated and at the end of my rope, I couldn't seem to figure it out. What was I missing in these courses, coaching programs, and books? I thought if I only knew the secret, then I could have amazing success. You might be feeling that same way right now.

If this sounds like you—if you have that itch on the back of your neck that you can't reach, no matter what you do—then you are in the right place. This book is for you. After years of frustration and pain, after countless hours of time lost, and after years of searching without finding, I have finally uncovered the greatest discovery of my life and I want to share it with you.

Our first lesson starts right now in this section. Each section will have a "Take Action" lesson where I will ask you to take action on what you've learned. Without action, what you learn will simply be knowledge. Knowledge is power, but knowledge without action is useless.

This may have happened to you before: You go to a seminar, get all pumped up from amazing content. You believe you are ready. You go home, take action for a day or two, and then it is back to the old way. This book is going to change that process.

Do you remember the title of this section? It's called:

"Your Internal Hero's Journey." The journey I'm referring to is your life, and I want you to be the hero in your own story. Master that internal mindset, and you will begin to see amazing things.

Why? Well, there is a powerful network of neurons in our brainstem that filters out all the unnecessary information so that only the important stuff gets through. It's called the Reticular Activating System or RAS. When it is activated, the mind focuses on what's important and creates a filter for it.

Don't believe me? Think about the last time you got a new car. What happened on the drive home?

Did you all of a sudden see that same type of car everywhere on the road? If so, you're not alone. It happened to me, and I was dumbfounded by it.

You may have asked yourself the question, "Did everyone start to drive this new car or buy it on the same day?" The answer is: No. Everyone didn't pick that day to drive the car, but your Reticular Activating System was triggered, so it created a filter for the car you recently purchased. Those cars were there all along, but your mind had no use for them, so your RAS had been filtering them out.

The same concept applies to your thoughts. If you are positive and focus on the good things, the brain will seek them out. I'm sure you have experienced a time when good things kept piling up in your day. With a smile on your face, shaking your head, you may have wondered, "How is this happening?"

On the flip side, if you focus on bad things, then your mind will narrow the focus to bring in more negativity. This creates that snowball effect to seek out all that is bad or negative in the world and let it into your mind.

When I learned how this works, a lightbulb went off in my head. I hope it did for you, too, because it is an amazing piece of knowledge to have an awareness about.

Now, let's get to work on triggering the RAS in our first Take Action section. I want you to go through the Take Action section and mentally feel it. This means closing your eyes and picturing yourself in the example.

As with anything that is worth doing, this is going to take practice and effort. When you feel yourself drift into old patterns or thoughts, go back to this exercise.

Take Action #1

I AM THE HERO IN MY OWN STORY

From now on, I want you to consider yourself the Hero in your Journey. Pick a comic book hero or someone you look up to or admire and step into that persona when needed.

I am a huge fan of the Marvel Cinematic Universe, so I typically choose Captain America or Thor as my two go-to personas or alter egos. One reason why I pick Thor is I have had a limiting belief that I was not worthy, so identifying with Thor helps me step out of those thoughts. More on that shortly.

Whoever it is, choose one so that when you need guidance or feel negative thoughts creep in, you can tap into that energy. This hero can be your alter ego when you need it most. When you need that extra push, get into that role, and show up like that person would show up.

Congrats on taking that first step!

IGNITE YOUR FIRE

Take time to document what you have learned and how it will apply to your life.

CHAPTER TWO

Every Fire Needs a Spark

Every fire starts with a spark. It can be a lightning bolt from the heavens (why I like the character Thor). Or it can be two rocks being rubbed together to create the first spark that ignites the kindling of a fire. Change in life takes a spark as well.

We (you and I as human beings) move for one of two reasons: either towards happiness/pleasure or away from pain. Let's dive into both and determine what will be your spark.

Why does pain cause you to move? What is it about pain that inspires action? Well, pain is uncomfortable and you want to get away from it. Our human minds at the core want to keep us safe and certain. If you are in pain, then you are definitely not safe and certain.

Think about a time when you have felt pain. When have you used pain as a spark to transform? Maybe it was a failed marriage, a bankrupt business, or the death of a loved one close to you.

The key factor is to let that pain drive you. To let it

burn and feel it, embrace all the suck of that pain. Remember those moments and how it felt so that you make a decision in your mind to never go back to that place.

How does it feel? Do feelings of hurt come to the surface? What does your body feel as you visualize the experience?

If you've had significant pain in your life, I want to tell you that I'm sorry you had to go through it. I will also tell you that if you use that pain to motivate you, it can be a great gift. You can use that negative and turn it into a positive.

Let's now examine the idea of pleasure for a moment. Pleasure is wanting or desiring some sort of outcome that gives you happiness and enjoyment. Maybe it's that house you've always wanted, a specific type of car, or the ability to put your kids through college. Explore your own feelings about what you desire most.

If you feel pleasure is going to be that driver for you, you need to visualize the desired outcome day in and day out. I would recommend putting up pictures of that future outcome all over your house as constant reminders of what you are working towards.

With each action you take, ask yourself: Is this taking me closer to what I want? The house, the car, whatever it might be. If it isn't, then you need to stop doing it and focus on things that move you closer to your desired goals. Don't give any energy to outcomes you don't desire.

Now that we've explored a bit of both pleasure and pain as motivators, it's important to choose one or the other. In my experience, the move from pain is the greater of the two. Let me explain with a story.

It was a cold December morning back in 2014, three days after Christmas. Just a normal day after the celebration of the holidays, when I'd typically start to think about what my goals, dreams, and aspirations would be for the upcoming year.

This particular morning started out like any other. I got in a workout and jumped in the shower. As I got out of the shower, I did what I would normally do on a Sunday morning during football season: I flipped on the TV to NFL gameday to get up to date on my beloved Philadelphia Eagles. I remember drying off while watching the TV when my phone rang.

Since it was a Sunday morning, I figured it was important, so I ran to the nightstand to grab my phone. I saw it was my dad, so I answered the phone, "Hey, Dad." As I heard his voice say, "Hello, Son," on the other line, all the hair on my arms stood up.

I could tell from his tone that something was wrong. My dad spoke in a soft, calm voice and said, "Your mom hasn't woken up in 24 hours. I think you need to get over here to the house." I told him I would be right there and that I loved him. I quickly got ready.

My mind raced with what the future would hold. I remember taking a few deep breaths to try to collect myself.

I was able to pull myself together enough to head downstairs to find my wife, Heather. I looked at her and she knew something was wrong. I told her that I had spoken to my dad, that my mom hadn't woken up for 24 hours, and that I needed to get over to the house. I hugged her with tears welling up in my eyes. I told her I loved her, and then I moved to my sons, Jackson and Carter.

Jackson was six and Carter was four at the time. I gave them both a tremendous bear hug, picked them up, and told them that I love them. I said, "I need to go see Grandmom." Tears started to stream down my face as I thought about how much my mom loved her grandchildren.

I collected my things and jumped in my truck to head to my parent's house about 20 minutes away. Time seemed to stand still as I drove. Memories flooded my mind. Thoughts of those Sunday dinners, Post-it® notes, and lucky pennies my mom used to give me whenever I had a big test or game (remember that for later).

My mom at this point was in hospice care for about two months. We knew her time was getting near. But you can never fully prepare yourself for the moment of passing. She had battled breast cancer on and off for 17 years. She fought hard every step of the way.

I don't think you can ever prepare yourself for life's beginning or end. Of course, we can't describe our own birth or death, but have you ever experienced the unconditional love and joy that comes with the birth of a child? Or have you ever known the searing pain and emptiness that comes from losing someone you love?

Birth and death are two experiences that people can try to describe, but they can't be fully grasped without living through them. Both experiences become imprinted on your soul.

I pulled into my parents' driveway. I grew up in that house. We moved there when I was five years old, and it had been our family's foundation for 34 years. I went into the house and up the stairs to my parents' room where my dad greeted me. I gave him a huge hug. With tears in his eyes, he told me he loved me. "I love you, too, Dad," I said.

As we released from the hug, I could see my sister Katie sitting on my parents' bed, holding my mom's hand. I walked over to the side of the bed, and Katie stood up. She looked at me with tears streaming down her face. We hugged and cried and whispered, "I love you," and "I love you, too."

I turned my attention to my mom, Judy. She lay peacefully on her bed. I watched her for a moment and listened to her take shallow breath after shallow breath. Taking her left hand in mine, I reached down to kiss her on her forehead. With tear-filled eyes, I whispered, "Mom, I'm here. I love you."

One thing my mom would always do when a friend, loved one, or anyone in her circle was going through a tough time was to send them a letter with the following quote that she adapted from something Charles Sawyer famously said:

> *"Of all the forces that make for a better world, none is so powerful as hope; with hope, one can think, one can work, one can dream. If you have hope, you have everything."*

Do you remember that Post-it® note when you first started reading this book? That is my gift to you. It is such a powerful statement for those that are in a time of need. You have my blessing, and I know my mother would love it if you use that in your own life in the future to impact others.

A few hours later my younger brother, Jon, got to the house. My mom must have sensed that her whole family was there—that all of her children were in her presence and in the house. It happened so suddenly, but we saw her gasp for air and then take her last breath as we all stood around her bedside.

The pain seared my heart. It felt like someone was actually standing on my chest. It was tough to breathe. I cried a cry that I had never cried before. If you've ever lost someone close to you, then you know how it feels.

Often in life, we will have a spark, but we won't know what it was or how it started our fire. I know losing my mom was my spark. It changed my life profoundly, and it propelled me to become who I was meant to be. Pain can be jet fuel to your dreams and goals.

Which will you choose? Tapping into a past pain or envisioning a future pleasure?

If you don't have past pain that you can tap into, here

is a quick strategy to project future pain. Think of where you will be in 10 years if you stay on the same path that you're on now. If nothing changes, what will the consequences be for you in two years? Five years? Ten years?

Maybe you're barely getting by and struggling financially day in day out, week after week. The thought of that frustration could be the spark that propels you forward. Explore your thoughts and jump into the next Take Action exercise.

Take Action #2

I want this to stick with you, so it will help you when you have hard days. Take the time right now to send me an email and cement that spark in your mind.

What I want you to send me is a brief description of the pain that will keep you going or the pleasure that you are chasing. It's a powerful thing when we speak out loud or put it down in written form. My email address is jeff@themorningfire.com. Ready, set, go.

I'm looking forward to hearing from you.

IGNITE YOUR FIRE

Take time to document what you have learned and how it will apply to your life.

CHAPTER THREE

Why We Stay Stuck

You are making great progress. Right now you should feel energy and purpose swell inside of you. You are now the hero in your journey and have found the source of pain or pleasure to pull you where you want to go.

The third step that has changed my world and my clients' world is to understand why we stay stuck. So many times, we work harder and harder in life. We feel like we are almost there ... as if it's just within our reach ... and then BAM! We fall back into what we are used to.

Does that sound all too familiar? It causes me to cringe when I write it. You're not alone. It's happened to all of us.

Here's the truth: it is not your fault. Yes, I feel like Robin Williams' character in *Good Will Hunting* when I say that to you, but it's true. It is not your fault.

Nothing in your education or growing up prepared you for success. It's not your fault. Release that heavy burden you might be carrying right now.

I realize this sounds utterly ridiculous, and trust me, I thought it *was* ridiculous the first time I did this, but bear with me. Through this process, I found hope and freedom—freedom from the weight I placed on myself daily—and I want you to feel that too.

Take Action #3

Take three deep breaths and say out loud: "It's not my fault." Say it with conviction so you feel it deep down in your soul. Scream it if you have to. Let it all out. How did it feel? Did you feel a lightness? If so, great; if not, do it again until you feel it.

Nice work! Now that you know it's not your fault, I want to be crystal clear that it is your responsibility to change it. No longer can you use that victim mentality. You are responsible for your future, and you are taking control of it today.

Here's the science behind it: Our mind has a limited number of calories it can use in a day, so anything and everything that our brain can automate and move to our subconscious mind, it will.

Think of your habits and rituals as those automated programs that run behind the scenes, like what happens when you boot up your computer or turn on your phone. Up to 95% of what we do is actually driven by our subconscious minds. Let that sink in for a quick second.

That means 95% of what we do we don't consciously think about. (Queue up the music again to the alarm clock scene in the movie *Groundhog Day*.) For that reason, it's no wonder why we stay stuck in an endless loop.

The second piece to the equation is that many of those habits and rituals are passed down in our families through generations. We adopt them as children because we want to be accepted and loved by our parents and those closest to us. As children, though, we weren't making conscious choices.

If we don't start to question those beliefs as adults, then we are destined to stay stuck. Typically, we have one or two limiting beliefs that play in our minds over and over again. As we put our foot on the gas pedal to get where we want to go, these limiting beliefs act as the other foot on the brake pedal, keeping us from gaining any real momentum or progress.

The two limiting beliefs that I have uncovered in myself are, "I'm not good enough," and "I'll never be successful." Those thoughts have played in my mind over and over again—subconsciously. Without me even realizing what's going on, those unquestioned assumptions have affected many of my decisions, killed my confidence, and driven many of my actions throughout much of my adult life.

Do you have one or two that you feel you have deep inside your subconscious mind? Maybe it's something you heard about related to money or success ... or maybe it was, "We are not morning people." Whatever it is, those subconscious beliefs have a hold on you right now and are limiting your growth.

Just 15 months ago, while writing this book, I found myself on a late winter morning, battling my mind. I was struggling in my business. It was not where I wanted it to be, and those negative thoughts were coming back with a vengeance.

They were telling me to quit, to give up, to throw in the towel, and move on. They said I wasn't good enough. They said I would never be successful.

I vividly remember driving down the road in my truck, gripping the steering wheel with both hands. Yelling at the top of my lungs, cursing and swearing and dropping F-bomb after F-bomb, I probably looked like a complete wacko to anyone who passed me that day.

What I was doing was trying to create some space from those negative thoughts—the thoughts that were gripping me and holding me back. With energy and passion, I was attempting to stop those negative thoughts at the door. It worked. A slight sliver of hope carried me through the rest of that day (and many more days to come). More on that story later.

Please know that every one of us has one or two negative thoughts. We always feel alone in our battles, but we are so similar. Have you ever thought to yourself, "Why am I the only one who feels this way?"

The truth is you are not alone. We all have self-sabotaging thoughts. Know that you are perfectly imperfect and that is the beauty of life and part of the journey.

You now have an awareness of what is driving your results. It's time to put on that white scientist lab coat and go to work to rewire your habits and rituals. You are going to hardwire them for success. What better place to start than when you first wake up in the morning? What you do when you first wake up matters more than you might think!

IGNITE YOUR FIRE

Take time to document what you have learned and how it will apply to your life.

CHAPTER FOUR

The Power of The Morning Routine

We often don't begin to change because we don't know where to start. Complexity is the killer of taking action. I follow a simple and straightforward approach that my coaching clients appreciate. They have seen tremendous results from it, and you can, too.

We are going to start with the morning routine and optimize it. This will light you up physically, mentally, and spiritually, laying the foundation for success.

If you think about how a house is built, what is the first step? Do the masons build brick upon brick on the sand? Absolutely not! The first step is to prepare a strong foundation so the house can stand against heavy winds and rain.

If you want tremendous success, a mansion of success, you had better build a rock-solid foundation. Your morning routine is that foundation.

Why the morning routine? Because as we sleep at night, our bodies rest. Physically and mentally we repair, heal, and recover from the day we've had. When you wake up, you are at a peak state to prime your system for your day, but, too often, here's what happens ...

Most of us play defense from the moment our alarm clocks go off. I coach both of my sons in basketball and I relate playing defense in life to playing defense on the basketball court. Your legs are bent and your quads begin to burn as you dig in to stop your opponent.

We are on defense and the day controls us. We play defense all day long, and we end the day exhausted. Feeling stressed with nothing left for our families or loved ones, we flop on the couch and throw on the TV. We think to ourselves, "How am I going to do this again tomorrow?"

Does that sound all too familiar? Have you ever felt or said to yourself, "I just can't do this again tomorrow"? If so, I'm thrilled that you are here because I can help you with exactly that.

From this point forward, you are going to control your day from the moment the alarm clock goes off. No longer are you going to hit that snooze button for eight extra minutes of non-quality sleep.

You are going to know exactly what to do when you wake up to create your Morning Fire that will drive your success. Your Morning Fire will positively impact all those around you. You will be a beacon of hope and energy.

This is the birth of your Morning Fire. The birth of the mantra is Rise, Fight, Love, Repeat. The mantra I live by day in day out. I want the same for you.

Take Action #4

Write down Rise, Fight, Love, Repeat on a notecard and keep it in your pocket. When you feel a lull in your day, I want you to reach into your pocket, feel that notecard, pull it out, and remember that is the simple formula to follow.

Now let's dive into what Rise, Fight, Love, Repeat is all about.

IGNITE YOUR FIRE

Take time to document what you have learned and how it will apply to your life.

CHAPTER FIVE

Discover the Rise

Each day we get on this Earth is a gift. I didn't realize that when I was younger, but I do now, years after my mother's passing. The Rise is the rebirth each morning filled with new opportunities and possibilities for your life.

You can create anything you want. How? Through the powerful choices you make throughout your day. Those choices and decisions build up over time, and they compound into results.

Before we get started focusing on how you will rise in the morning, I want you to think about preparing the night before. The legendary coach John Wooden said, "Failure to prepare is preparing to fail." I want you to think about how you wake up in the morning.

Are you prepared with everything set out and ready to go? If not, that's step one. Prepare the night before so you are ready as the gun sounds off at the starting line of your morning. Clothes out, mess cleaned up, lunches made for the kids if you have children.

The next step is to pre-program your mind so you feel

a certain way when you wake up. Prepare your mind for the number of hours you will sleep and the time at which you will rise. We are prepping the mind with those thoughts to mull over as you sleep.

Go to bed with intention. Before you fall asleep, say to yourself *out loud*, "I will wake up with energy, focus, and passion. I will be getting six hours of sleep and waking up at 4:00 AM. This is exactly what my mind, body, and soul need."

Yes, I know what you may be thinking: Man, this guy makes me say things out loud a whole heck of a lot. Well, if I knew it wouldn't make a difference, I wouldn't tell you to do it. But here's the thing: The spoken word unleashes power which causes your mind and the universe to follow what you say. It's important to proclaim out loud what you want—the outcomes you desire.

Now, from this point forward, as you wake up in the morning, I want you to envision the Phoenix rising from the ashes reborn and ready to fly. Close your eyes right now and picture it.

What did it look like? Did it have huge wings as it rose out of the fire? This is how you will wake up tomorrow morning if you follow my guidance.

When I imagine the Phoenix rising, I also imagine music playing in the background, like a scene from a movie. I get a surge of energy from it. As the Phoenix rises in my mind, hope rises in my spirit. You can experience that same triggered response if you practice this visualization over time.

So how do we Rise in the morning? This is a critical question to ask ourselves—especially if we've been in the habit of playing defense from the moment our alarm goes off.

Unfortunately, when the alarm goes off, we often hit the snooze button. Are you a habitual snooze button presser? I used to hit the snooze button two times before I would get up. I actually set my alarm so I could get up earlier and then hit the snooze.

Are you with me? I know I can't be alone. If you struggle with the snooze button, here's a strategy to defeat that snooze button once and for all. It's a groundbreaking concept on the cutting edge of science (queue the sarcasm).

If you hit the snooze button and want to break that habit, you must put your phone away from your bed. That's it, simple and straightforward.

Put in a place where you physically have to get out of those warm covers to turn it off. The fact that you hit the cold air and move in those split seconds while you are going to turn off the alarm drastically increases your chances that you will get moving once you get up.

Also, just so you know about that precious snooze sleep time, studies show that the snooze sleep you get does not help you feel any more refreshed and actually may make you more tired. Sleep cycles are 90 minutes in length, so try to plan out your sleep accordingly. I get six hours of sleep a night or four sleep cycles.

Lay out your clothes for the morning right beside your

phone. This will be another signal that it's time to get up and start your morning routine. Here's why: Your mind will take the easy way out every day and twice on Sundays. If you aren't prepared, it will throw roadblocks up and tell you to go climb back into that warm bed.

Have you ever wanted to get up early, so you set your alarm, but when you got up, you couldn't find your favorite pair of shorts or favorite shirt? As you went back to bed, maybe you thought to yourself, "It's a sign that I shouldn't get up." I call BS. It was your mind taking the easy way out.

We are showing our minds that we are in control. We prepare to win the morning and will stop at nothing to achieve it. When you start in control, the whole frequency of your day changes. Your posture, your mood, your attitude will all change.

The second part of the Rise is all about hydration. I want you to drink a full glass of water when you immediately wake up. That glass of water should be out and available for you, or, if you use a water bottle, it should be full and ready to go. This is vital to starting to wake up the body, mind, and spirit to give it what it needs.

You get dehydrated overnight and your body is craving that water when you first get up. 60% of the adult body is made of water. 73% of the brain and heart are composed of water. The lungs are at a staggering 83%. Do you think water is important to how you operate?

Yes, it absolutely is! The longest time we go without drinking water is overnight. If you are going to the kitchen to get your glass of water in the morning, I want it already poured and ready to go when you get there. Why? Well, in the same way you laid out your clothes next to your phone, you need to set out your water.

This is another opportunity for your mind to stop you in your tracks. If you reach into the cabinet and your favorite glass isn't there, or there are no glasses, your mind will guide you to take the easy way out and tell you to forget it. This happens all the time throughout your day.

Take Action #5

Put your phone away from your bed so you physically have to get out of bed to turn it off. Have your phone next to your clothes so it gives you that mental signal to get up. Lastly, have that full glass of water or water bottle waiting for you so you can get rehydrated right away.

IGNITE YOUR FIRE

Take time to document what you have learned and how it will apply to your life.

CHAPTER SIX

Bring the Fight

From an early age, growing up with siblings, I was told not to fight. I was the oldest of three and have a younger brother three years younger. I can still remember my mom yelling at me to stop fighting with my brother. The same thing happens with my sons today.

Think back to your childhood. If you have a sibling, remember the days that your parents told you not to fight. Eventually, those warnings wore you down as a kid and you stopped fighting. Even worse, you may have been sent to your room to face the consequences. Do these words sound familiar? "You're grounded from fighting."

If you were an only child, what about at school? Were you told by your teachers to break it up and stop fighting? If so, then those messages subconsciously wore you down.

There is a great story that one of my mentors, Tony Robbins, tells about an elephant in the circus. This elephant is brought into the tent as a baby. The handlers drive a stake into the ground and chain the baby elephant to the stake. The baby elephant fights and fights to try to get away, but it eventually gives up.

The baby elephant stops fighting. As the elephant grows, it becomes physically capable of ripping out that stake, but because it has been conditioned to believe it's impossible, it doesn't even try.

Could that be what happens to us growing up? I think we have all faced that kind of conditioning. While it's true that we shouldn't be beating on anyone, it's also true that in our formative years, our fighting instincts are muted or stopped. Powers of authority (our parents, teachers, or coaches) have driven an invisible stake in the ground and chained our Fight to it.

I want you to unlearn all that was taught to you. Now, I'm not saying to go start getting in fights with anyone and everyone around you. What I am saying is we need to uncover that fight mentality that has layers upon layers of conditioning on top of it.

Think back to your dreams right now as a kid. Maybe you wanted to have a million dollars, play in the NBA (just me?), live in a huge mansion, drive a fancy sports car, or become famous. My question is: When did you become conditioned like the elephant that you don't even try anymore?

Unfortunately, if you are like me, we let ourselves off the hook. We say we want it, but then we settle for what we are used to. We say to ourselves, "It's okay not to fight with everything I have in me just to get what I want." We lose that fight mentality, and it creates space for us to believe that it's okay to be average.

My question to you is: Are you okay with being average? When I read that sentence, the inner lion inside of me yells, "HELL, NO!" That inner lion inside needs to be unleashed. That lion needs to break free from the chains and be set free to fight.

As we wake in the morning, too often we rely on stimulants to give us the energy we need to start the day. We already whipped that damn snooze button and have a path to start our day. Now it's time to rev up the engine that is our body.

How are we going to do that? We are going to do that through movement. Movement for energy is critical to wake up your body, so you can tackle whatever comes your way throughout your day.

Think about a day when it's really cold out and you start your car. Do you just start the car and go? Absolutely not! You need to start the car, let it warm up, and then it will operate at peak performance. In the same way, your body is like that car (it may help to imagine your body as a Ferrari or Lamborghini or some other fancy sports car).

Your Morning Fire routine needs to have exercise as a component. You are fighting for your physical fitness. You are revving up your engine for energy. Ten minutes of movement in some fashion is all it takes, and it doesn't even need to be an exercise to burn calories.

It can be going for a walk for 10 minutes and breathing fresh air. It can be doing some stairs in your house or doing core work. Once you get through 10 minutes, your blood will be flowing and you will have energy that you thought you needed coffee and caffeine to generate. Please note I'm not against a good cup of Joe but what I am against is being reliant on the caffeine to get you going in the morning.

Plus, if you want to have the ability to tackle everything life throws at you, then you need to be in shape, simple and straightforward. Regardless of where you are in your journey, 10 minutes in the morning can start that process and take your energy level to new heights.

Case in point, I recently had a client of mine lose 10 pounds by working out for 10 minutes a day in my Morning Fire Academy 10-week coaching program. It honestly blew his mind since he thought he needed to be in the gym for hours to get in shape.

The key was that he was consistent over 70 days. He worked out every single day, which was the longest stretch of his life he had ever worked out consistently. It was amazing to be part of his journey and see his results.

Now that you have the engine that is your body awake and primed for the day, you'll need to focus on the fuel that you put in your body. If your body is an expensive sports car, what type of octane would you put in one of those cars? Would you put the regular 87 octane gas into it?

Absolutely not!

So why do we do it to our own bodies?

If you are eating a high-sugar/high-fat breakfast such as muffins, donuts, or highly processed cereals, you are basically destroying your sports car from the inside out. It might work for now, but eventually, it will break down and no longer run at the speed that you want it to.

It's critical to get some good fuel into your body when you start your morning. I recommend doing this through the green smoothie. Did you know that only one in 10 adults eats the proper amount of fruit and vegetables per day?

How many servings of fruits and vegetables do you get in a day? Be honest, no lying about it. I know I struggled for years getting enough fruits and vegetables in my system.

For vegetables, that is two to three cups of vegetables per day; for fruit, it is one and a half to two cups per day. Now, if you incorporate the green smoothie into your routine, you will be well on your way to your targets before most people roll out of their warm, snug beds in the morning. And by most people, I'm talking about the 9 out of 10 who aren't getting enough fruits and vegetables.

Crazy how small little steps can put you ahead of the game. Too often, we think we need to make these grand, sweeping changes, but if we make small tweaks here and there, those small tweaks can have a profound impact on our life and results over time. Back to the smoothie.

As the foundation for my smoothie, I love frozen green

vegetables such as spinach and kale along with a banana. I highly recommend some chia seeds as well to provide the mind with some good fats for fuel in the morning. It might take some getting used to, but with commitment, you'll be surprised at how your body eventually starts to crave the good stuff. You'll also be surprised at the profound impact it has on your energy levels and your ability to stay focused.

Become that scientist in your white lab coat and play around with what you like or dislike in your smoothie. Drop me a line at jeff@themorningfire.com and I'll send you my latest smoothie recipe.

We've primed the engine that is our body, check. Put optimal fuel in the engine, check.

We have one last critical piece to the puzzle. This is by far the most important one and should not be taken lightly because so much of what we do is a battle in our mind. The toughest battle you will ever fight is the battle within yourself.

I spent decades in this battle with no ally or friend there to help me. There were countless battles that I lost over and over again. But here's the key point I want you to consider.

If you continue to lose battle after battle, but you keep getting back up, do you think you will ever win the war? Will your mind eventually say, "There's no stopping this person, so we might as well go all-in"?

I'm here to tell you yes. Your mind will yield, and once you begin to build those muscles, amazing things will open up to you, but let me be clear. This is also a never-ending battle that you will need to continue to fight.

This is a journey, and once you stop doing the daily work, those negative, self-defeating thoughts, along with bad habits, will creep back in, so you must fight every single day.

The third piece of the Fight is meditation. When you hear that word, you might visualize exactly what I used to visualize: a bald monk in a robe with his legs crossed and eyes closed, sitting on the side of a huge mountain in silence.

Did you think the same thing? It's okay, I have been there and done that. I thought meditation was very woo-wooish, but, boy was I wrong. I dabbled with meditation for a while, but then I made a commitment to do it every day regardless of where I am or what I am doing.

Making that commitment and tracking it can be a game-changer for you. I've now meditated 10 minutes a day for 900+ straight days as of writing this book and I'm not stopping anytime soon.

Why is it a game-changer? For one, you are bombarded by countless distractions all day long. To be able to spend 10 minutes focusing on your breath and calming your mind can be incredibly beneficial to you mentally and spiritually.

You might have picked up on a reoccurring theme that I've been putting down in this book so far. The theme is creating small habits that are achievable. I'm not talking about meditating on the side of a mountain for two hours. I'm talking about finding a quiet, dark place to close your eyes and listen to a guided meditation app to create some space in your mind for 10 minutes.

If 10 minutes is too much, try one or two minutes and then build up over time. While this is a blueprint, I also understand we are all beautifully unique human beings.

Add this to your routine, and you will have hit the Fight "Big 3." You will have fought for your physical, nutritional, and mental fitness. You will feel a surge in your body, mind, and soul that kickstarts your day.

I will give you a warning though. The people around you are going to wonder what the heck you are doing. They may ask you questions about why you are jumping around with energy and a smile on your face this early in the morning. Don't let them throw shade your way. Instead, reply, "I am living life to the fullest and grateful for today."

Take Action #6

Write down what you are going to do tomorrow for exercise, research green smoothie recipes, and download a meditation app that you can use for your meditation practice. Insight timer is my favorite app for meditation.

Remember that story I was telling about when my mind was kicking my ass 15 months ago, and I was yelling at myself in my truck? After that episode, I went to the church I grew up in. It's the church where my mom is buried in the cemetery out back.

I was headed there to meet with a preschool director since the gym I own runs preschool fitness classes there. I met with the director, and we got to talking about the next year for her students.

I was passionate and full of energy as I love guiding children not only in physical fitness but also in life. At the end of the conversation, Karen said to me, "You were meant to come here today." It took me by surprise, so I asked her, "Why?"

She said, "Because I lost my dad three months ago and I haven't worked out or taken time for myself since then, but tomorrow I am going to." We had tears in our eyes as I hugged her and told her that her sharing that story meant so much to me.

That encounter started my thinking that maybe, just maybe, I was on the right path. I was beginning to come out of my funk, but more to come on that story later.

IGNITE YOUR FIRE

Take time to document what you have learned and how it will apply to your life.

CHAPTER SEVEN

Love Yourself

One of the basic fundamental needs we have as human beings is to be loved. Many times, we do things that might not really align with who we are in an attempt to be accepted and to be loved. We can all remember when we have felt that overwhelming sense of love, maybe it was from a parent, a child, or our significant other.

It brought us joy and happiness that we wanted to hold onto with both of our hands and never let go. We have a basic fundamental need for love, which I find quite ironic.

Why?

Because so many times we do not love ourselves.

We are the harshest critic for what we didn't do, for the call we didn't make, for the opportunity we didn't take advantage of, for the shot we didn't take, for the mistake we made on the project.

We as human beings are inherently hard on ourselves and we beat ourselves up. My question for you is: Do you love yourself?

Today, right here, that self-destructive and negative self-image thought-pattern ends. I want you to begin to love yourself with all of your heart. Are you perfect? No, but no one is.

Celebrate that uniqueness and know that you are where you are right now because that is where you are meant to be. I'm going to ask you to do something very powerful in this take action exercise. It might bring you to tears as it did for me some years ago, but it can unlock an awareness and love that you most likely haven't felt in years.

Take Action #7

I want you to go into a room with a mirror. I want you to stand in front of the mirror and close your eyes. Then, I want you to take five deep breaths.

When you are done with that fifth breath, I want you to open your eyes and stare right into your own eyes in that mirror. It may be uncomfortable at first, but trust the process.

Staring into your own eyes, I want you to say to yourself three times: "I love you." Let all the emotion out as you release any past pain or failures in your life.

Take the time to really stare at yourself and love yourself. You are amazing!

How did that feel? Did emotions unexpectedly grab you? Were you surprised by what came out all of a sudden from within? I remember being in tears as I said those words to myself.

It's a grounding exercise that you can do to give yourself love, grace, and power. Congratulations on taking action. I know how difficult that exercise can be. I want you on a daily basis to be grateful for who you are and all the gifts that you have to give the world.

There is an amazing thing that happens when you love yourself. What happens? You love all those around you more. You show up more for the people who are most important to you.

How can you do that? Write them a note or send them a text today. Don't wait for tomorrow. Tell them how grateful you are to have them in your life. Maybe it's someone who made a difference in your life at some point. Reach out to that person and tell them how grateful you are.

Feeling grateful and spreading that gratitude will fill you up with such joy that you'll want to continue to reach out to people on a daily basis. These expressions of love will provide perspective for the challenging or difficult moments you're bound to face. You'll discover that more and more, you'll find appreciation for all that life has to offer.

I enjoy sending five texts or voice messages on a Friday to people in my circle telling them how grateful I am to have them in my life. The responses I have gotten back are amazing, from "you just made my day," to much longer, inspirational texts like this one from my uncle: "You cannot be happy focused on yourself. You were made for Mission. It's deep within you. Only, ONLY by serving others in a meaningful way do we truly discover the happiness we yearn for so unrelentingly."

Taking a few seconds out of your day to spread love can make a world of difference. It will also fill your heart up with joy and gratitude, which is a powerful way to exist and live. The world needs love now more than ever.

IGNITE YOUR FIRE

Take time to document what you have learned and how it will apply to your life.

CHAPTER EIGHT

Repeat to Greatness

I've shared the importance of Rise, Fight, and Love, but without the last piece to the puzzle, all that you have learned won't matter much in the end. See, if you do things only a few times, you most likely won't get much in the way of results. I don't want that for you.

I know you don't want that either; otherwise, you wouldn't have gotten this book and read it to this point (P.S., if you are still reading to this point, thank you). I want you to get long-lasting results from reading this book when you implement the strategies that I discuss.

That's why the gold is in the Repeat. I'm not sure where I heard it, but I love the line: "Repetition is the tunnel to greatness." It's not sexy at all and can feel completely monotonous at times, but there is beauty in it.

Remember how, at the beginning of the book, I shared how much of what we do is on autopilot? Approximately 95% of what we do is driven by our habits and rituals. By repeating your practice over and over, you will develop new habits and rituals to unlock your potential.

I'll bet you've heard somewhere that it takes 21 days to create a habit. Whoever said that took the bare minimum amount of time and marketed the concept pretty darn well because everyone knows it and fully believes it.

If you take a look at your local gym, though, by the third week in January, you know that it can't possibly be 21 days to create a habit because the parking lot is back to where it usually is. Those New Years' resolution clients have fallen off the wagon.

Here's why:

Recently, studies have shown through brain scans that habits are formed anywhere from 21 to 67 days. They actually looked at the neural pathways of the habits firing in the brain. Right before 21 days, those old habits dig in and fight like hell to stop you from creating that new habit because if you do, the old habit will die on the vine and break up.

The 21-day concept gives people false hope. They believe that at 21 days, they've made it! In reality, though, this is the time for them to bare down and push through. It's why my group coaching program is 10 weeks or 70 days—to get past that 67-day mark and ensure those habits and rituals stick.

I realize it goes against everything you have heard, learned, and were taught growing up, but I am a firm believer in it, and if you think of that gym parking lot scenario or anytime you have tried to create a habit that sticks, you understand it to be true.

Right now, you might be saying: Great. It takes longer than I thought to create a habit, so this is going to take hard work. My answer? A plain and simple: Yes.

Listen, we all want that magic pill. The pill that strips off weight or shreds us with muscle. That one thing to turn our finances around. But anyone who is successful will tell you there was no magic pill. They achieved the results they desired through flat out hard work.

In my 45 years on this Earth, I have had to learn the hard way through many failures, heartbreaks, and financial collapses that nothing replaces consistent, persistent work.

There's a saying that I love from motivational speaker Les Brown: "Do what is easy and your life will be hard. Do what is hard and your life will become easy." The good news is there are some strategies to get you there that I'll share with you now.

Have you ever had this happen in your life? You have something new you want to start doing. You are all juiced up and ready to go, but you keep it to yourself. You start for a couple of days, then you stop.

You are filled with regret because you let yourself down and you beat yourself up. You struggle with the question: "Why did I fail?" or "Why did I fail again?"

The answer is you didn't know the right strategy, or you didn't get help. By getting help, I mean making your intentions public.

It's easy to let yourself off the hook. The mind will take the easy way out every time it's given an opportunity. Remember learning that in the Rise section?

If you fail, no one knows but you. Then, you have to deal with that feeling of failure and regret. But if you announce it on social media, tell your friends, or share it with your family, something magical happens. A small, subtle switch occurs in your mind that you won't even be aware of, which will drive you toward success.

What happens is you don't want to look like a liar to your network, family, or friends. This is a powerful force that you can leverage to your advantage. I used it recently, and the pull that it had was nothing short of amazing.

I went public that I would go live on Facebook at 12:30 PM for a full month. Now, no one was going to hold me accountable, no one at the end of the day would care if I didn't go live, there wasn't going to be a public shaming if I didn't complete the task, but deep down I wanted to be a man of my word and it drove me.

There were weekend days when it was sunny and 75 degrees out when the last thing I wanted to do was go live at 12:30, but I did it every single day. I even took my laptop with me on trips, set up a hotspot from my phone, and went live in a parking lot. We all have this deep-seated need to be consistent with our word to others and true to what we say in public.

Putting that mind hack into action can have a tremendous impact on your success.

Take Action #8

Create a social media post and make it public what time you will be waking up starting tomorrow and how long you will be doing it for. Make it as specific as possible because clarity will help hold you accountable.

For example, if you say, "Tomorrow, I am going to wake up 30 minutes earlier," no one can hold you accountable because they may not be aware of when you wake up now. Instead say, "Starting tomorrow, I will be waking up at 5:00 AM for the next 30 days and completing my Morning Fire Routine." Tag me in the post so I know you have taken action. My Instagram handle is @jeff_wickersham or you can find me on Facebook at facebook.com/jeffrey.wickershm.

Before I wrap up this section, I want to share two quick concepts with you. The first is from a book I read called *Infinite Game* by Simon Sinek. In the book, Sinek says, "Consistency becomes more important than intensity" (p. 24). Basically, the concept states that if you continue doing the work, day in and day out, without a shadow of a doubt, you will be successful.

You don't know when you will be successful, but, eventually, you will be. Take a moment to let that sink in and write it down so you can go back and read it when you feel your mind begin to waver.

The second concept has to do with repetition and is more visual in nature. Hypothetically speaking, let's say that I go to my backyard to plant some Chinese bamboo seeds.

The next night, while watering my seeds, I see my neighbor, and he asks what I'm doing. I tell him I planted some seeds, and I'm dedicated to helping them grow by watering them daily. He has a garden in his backyard, so he says he can't wait to see them grow.

I religiously water for a week, then a month, then three months, and then I see my neighbor out back again and he lets me know that they should have been showing some signs of growth. Maybe they didn't take. Maybe I should give up. I let him know that it takes time, but I will stick with it.

One year passes. No growth. But I remain committed to my cause. Two years, three years, four years pass. By now, my family is wondering whether I have lost my mind as each night I go out to nurture, water, and tend to my seeds.

No one would blame me at this point if I gave up. My

children ask me what I'm doing. Even though I have become the butt of some neighborhood jokes, I stay committed.

In the fifth year, something amazing happens. The Chinese bamboo breaks through the ground and I rejoice. Everyone who thought I was crazy is now amazed by it. The bamboo doesn't merely grow—it explodes in growth and ends up growing 80 feet in the air in only six weeks! Truly amazing growth, but also a heck of a story of perseverance, patience, consistency, and faith.

Why do I share that story? Well, many times in your hero's journey, you are going to be tested. You are going to have those around you who think it's time to give up, but what I will tell you is this: You never know when you are going to break through that soil and sprout up 80 feet in the air in six weeks.

We think there will be a straight-line path in growth, but there are some things in nature that don't grow that way—like the Chinese bamboo. If you believe in your mission, your passion, and your vision, then repetition will get you there even if your path ends up being that of the bamboo.

IGNITE YOUR FIRE

Take time to document what you have learned and how it will apply to your life.

CHAPTER NINE

Putting All the Pieces Together

It's time to tie up the loose ends, dot the I's, and cross the T's. Let's get you ready to embark on your hero's journey. Take a moment to smile from ear to ear. Feel that happiness roll over your shoulders. The majority of people don't ever take time for themselves the way you have.

Did you know that the average adult reads only three books in their lifetime? You are certainly not average, and you deserve to be celebrated.

Many times in life we wait for what we think we need before we get started. We wait for circumstances, environment, motivation, and mindset to be perfect before we start, trying to ensure our success before we kick it into gear.

Have you ever delayed starting something until another day because you said, "I need to wait for this day because of X, Y, or Z?" I know I have in my life. I waited three months before I built my course because I thought it was going to be too difficult. Once I started,

I couldn't believe the time I had wasted, not realizing I was more than capable.

I know a lot of people do that related to a new diet or exercise regimen. They might decide on a Thursday to change their eating habits or workout routine, and they feel motivated to start, but they think, "Give me one more weekend to eat like crap, sleep late, and I will start on Monday when I am motivated and can start fresh."

How has that worked out? Usually, they're not successful because their mind got in the way and stopped them.

You need to take action *now*.

The fact is that motivation, inspiration, and willpower are limited resources. The key to getting more of each is action. When you take action, your mind feels you moving, can sense you are going in the right direction, and through that little taste of success, you are motivated and inspired to do more.

It creates this amazing triangle of:

Action → Motivation → Inspiration

... that continues to build on itself. This is a very important concept to understand and put into practice. Taking action will inspire and motivate you, so *just take action.*

Second, we as humans have this belief that we will be good at something right out of the gate when we start something new. This almost always isn't the case. You will suck when you start something new.

It's a harsh reality, but if you understand and realize it, you will be more likely to move forward. Your mindset needs to be that you will get better over time with practice, hard work, and determination. Have you ever started something new, weren't good at it, and then just gave up?

That is the old you. The new you will continue to work and get better.

I remember when I first launched my Morning Fire podcast. Looking back, I sucked when I started, but how could I not? I was doing something I had never done before with no experience whatsoever. When I relistened to those first episodes after I published #300, I cringed listening to myself speak, but that's okay. It's about the journey and continuing to develop every single day.

When you think or believe that you need to be perfect, it will cause you to stop. Perfection equals paralysis in my book, and if you are in that perfection mindset, I'm sure you have stopped taking action on something because it didn't feel right to you.

My advice is to take action, understand it will be messy, but learn from it and continue to grow. If you trust the process, great things will happen for you. Act as if your success is guaranteed and watch how you will show up.

Third, define your mindset and then shift it towards

the growth side of the fence. There are two mindsets: a growth mindset and a fixed mindset. In her book *Mindset,* Carol Dweck does a great job of defining them (so good, in fact, that I have read her book not once but twice!)

A growth mindset is one where you believe you can get better at anything with practice, hard work, and repetition. You see difficulties as opportunities to grow and that any road bump or failure is part of the process. You search out new things that are challenges because you know that those experiences will make you better.

I like to relate this mindset to a book that my mom always used to read to me. It was called *The Little Engine That Could*. The famous line in that book is: "I think I can, I think I can, I think I can."

A fixed mindset is one where you believe you have been given certain traits, skills, or abilities and they cannot be changed. You believe that you were born a certain way and that is just the way it is. If you have ever said, "That is just the way I am," then you are exhibiting the fixed mindset.

Oftentimes, when I speak with people and I talk about the morning routine, they tell me they are just not a morning person, that they were just born that way.

I always like to pose the question:

Do you think when you were born, the nurses, the doctor, or your creator stamped you on the head and said you are not a morning person?

Absolutely not!

(Feel free to use this question in the future if you ever feel yourself getting trapped into that fixed mindset.)

What is more likely is that the "I'm not a morning person" belief is something you learned, heard, or adopted from those closest to you that you now believe is in your DNA.

Search your thoughts and feelings to determine what side you fall on from a mindset perspective. Then, work to make a switch to that growth mindset, believing anything is possible, that you can reach that next level of success through hard work, determination, and belief. I believe in you and all the gifts you have.

Lastly, I want you to burn the boats. I want you to play all out and become who you were born to be. Be that hero in the story that is your life. The concept of burning the boats can be very powerful.

My mentor, Tony Robbins, speaks to it quite often. Burning the boats is a concept that comes from the history of the Vikings, who were amazing warriors. Not only were they trained physically as warriors, but they also had a mental approach that caused them to go all-in.

When the Vikings would sail to a far-off land with the intent to capture a particular island, the captains would wait for everyone to get ashore and then issue the command: *Burn the boats!* The Viking warriors had one of two options: either win the war or die in the process. There was no retreat. No going back to the boats.

Imagine if you were a Viking with children and a spouse at home. How do you think you would show up to fight? If you're anything like the Vikings, you would fight like there was no tomorrow so you could see your family again.

It was that mental shift that enabled them to fight all-out. It forced them to give every ounce of their body, being, and soul to the battle. You can make that mental shift as well.

I want you to burn the boats and go all in. I want you to focus on the power of the morning routine for more energy, focus, abundance, and time in your life. Each day to Rise, Fight, Love, Repeat.

I know it can propel you to that next level of success that you have always wanted. It can be your blueprint and competitive advantage that most people don't focus on. Fortunately for you, you are not like most people.

You are that superhero you first established in Section One, that hero in your own journey. Step into that role and believe in yourself like your success is guaranteed.

Take Action #9

Community is such a key to success. For that reason, I created a private FB group called Rise, Fight, Love, Repeat where you can continue to be inspired, motivated, and get access to the community of like-minded people who have read the book.

Request access to the group here: https://www.facebook.com/groups/RiseFightLoveRepeat/

Now to finish my story of 15 months ago when my mind was kicking my ass, I screamed at the top of my lungs to get some space, and then met with a woman who said I was meant to come there that day.

I was still struggling but had some twinges in my mind that even though I was at a very low point, signs were popping up to guide me. I went out back to the cemetery to my mom's gravesite. On that day, the only thing I wanted was a hug from my mom.

Sobbing, I asked her if it would all be okay. I asked her if I was on the right path. I longed to hear her positive message of hope and inspiration.

I knelt down and cleaned her tombstone and told her that I loved her. I told her that I knew she watched over me and will always be there for me in spirit. I kissed my hand and then pressed it to her name.

Standing up, I started on my way, but I continued to battle those thoughts. They had diminished from where they started, but I was still left with this uneasy question: Am I on the right path?

Later that night, I went to change out the laundry from the washer to the dryer. I felt like the only one who knows how to clean the lint out of the dryer. Are you with me on that one?

As I reached down to grab the lint out of the filter, I could not believe my eyes. I instantly got goosebumps all over my body. I shook my head, smiled, and started to tear up.

I yelled to my wife who was in the next room to come and take a look. She knew that I was having a really tough day. I said, "Look at this," and I showed her the lint filter. A lucky penny was staring back at us.

I pointed to the heavens and smiled. From that moment on, I knew I was on the right path. I wouldn't waiver in my purpose or convictions ever again. That penny was a hug from my mom letting me know that everything would be okay.

So many times in life we question where we are headed. We want to see what is going to happen in front of us, to know the outcome. Unfortunately, we cannot connect the dots forward, only backward.

I hope my story of pain and signs was confirmation that you need to have faith and trust in yourself.

Eventually, when you look back, you will be able to connect all the dots.

Your future begins with every morning you wake up and Ignite Your Morning Fire.

Rise, Fight, Love, Repeat. Get after it!

IGNITE YOUR FIRE

Take time to document what you have learned and how it will apply to your life.

Client Success Stories

"Instead of Rise, Fight, Love, Repeat, my life was rise, survive, hide, repeat. All my efforts were spent staying safe and secure. It was suffocating me and my family. I'm a very different person today because of you. I cannot thank you enough. Morning Fire has had a profound impact on my life. My kids love the notes I put in their lunches. They say their friends look forward to them too. I'm happier than ever and more confident than ever! No longer satisfied to just survive, I want to thrive. I'm becoming the leader and role model my children deserve, the person I was meant to be. Thank you for giving me hope, for helping me believe that I can overcome these so-called demons that have been holding me back."

— Jason, Collegeville, PA

"I have experienced a new lease on life, breaking bad habits, relating to others, and seeing first-hand what others were going through and the goals they have. I have learned to limit the time on my phone, get myself up and out of bed each day with a positive attitude. I have learned to set goals and rewire my thinking and to be grateful for each day even if it's not perfect. I am the only one who has the ability to make the most out of my life."

— Leslie, Audubon, PA

"I recently jumped into the Morning Fire program after being in a slump in my life and workouts. Since then, I have never looked back. The simplicity and discipline have given me what I need to work on myself daily. I love the focus and energy it has given me."

— Tara, Charleston, SC

"I did the program, and it completely transformed not only how I approach my day but also how I can be engaged and productive. This past 12 months I went through some personal stuff that was the most challenging time of my life. Without the Morning Fire, I would not have been able to get through it and be intact. The program is a perfect way to get focused and grow."

— Greg, Sandy Spring, MD

"I loved the support from Jeff and the group, accountability with the group. Great direction, easy to follow. Leadership from Jeff and others. The routine is great, but you have to buy in completely. You have to want the results and put in the effort. Like most things, if you don't put in the effort, you will not get the desired result. It's up to you...but all the support really helps and keeps you on track, keeps you motivated."

— Anonymous Client

"What the Morning Fire taught me was discipline and doing things on a consistent basis can get you to have good habits. Thank you, Jeff Wickersham, for the program as it has really helped me and I can't wait to continue."

— Kaushika, Collegeville, PA

"I have rheumatoid arthritis, and I could sleep all day long. With this program, I have discovered newfound energy compared to when I have usually crashed. I'm getting excited for the possibilities that are now out there for my future."

— Karen, Collegeville, PA

"All I can really say is THANK YOU for allowing me to part of this process. It has gotten me back on the right track with taking care of myself and feeling good about life. I was always a guy who worked out in my 20s to mid-30s, and I had just recently dabbled in meditating before starting your program. I had even started reading some self-help books in the past 3-4 years because I was struggling to be positive.

"Through the books and meditating, I have learned that so much of what I do as a human being comes from within, so any workouts I missed or videos I didn't watch were my own doing...not the program. What I liked about your program is it helped to bring a lot of the things I was trying to piece-meal together into one place with the workouts, the meditating, and the positive podcasts. I am definitely a better person because of it!!!

"Jeff, you are a genuine guy (which is hard to find in today's world), and you are an inspiration to me. I sincerely appreciate you allowing me the opportunity to be part of this start-up process. I wish you all the success in the world and THANK YOU again for helping me to become a better person."

— Tom, Philadelphia, PA

"I enjoyed the very well-organized, thought-through process with a straight-forward roadmap to follow. I loved the team atmosphere and having Jeff as a leader has been so inspiring. I'm so happy to have developed a habit that I can't imagine my mornings without now. My morning routine makes me a better person all around. I look forward to keeping up practicing, growing, and gaining more energy and reaching new goals."

— Anonymous Client

"The idea that with everything going on in our world there was one thing that was completely in my control which is how I go about starting my day. It's a time of zero distractions and total time to myself and what I need to get done for myself to get the day started right. It was the perfect opportunity to get myself ready as the best version of myself for everyone else."

— Brian, York, PA

"I love the energy level it created, Jeff's positivity, and the workouts. I think the program is great for people who have a hard time staying motivated, organized, or getting to work on time. The organizational tips to streamline the morning routine are a nice touch. Jeff is a really great guy and his positivity really makes the program."

— Andrew, Morgantown, PA

"The Morning Fire Academy is an excellent foundation for teaching you to live in the present. Rise, Fight, Love, Repeat is actually a good catchphrase that has become the backbone of my daily life. The recommendations that are provided by Jeff can give a good foundation to those that may not have a good structure to start their day."

— Chris, Jeffersonville, PA

"I enjoyed the very prescriptive approach with the videos and instruction. It was very personal and easy to follow. I love the new ideas I was able to incorporate into my life. Affirmations, notes/messages to my wife and kids, meditation."

— Kory, Phoenixville, PA

"The morning fire has done two things for me. It has brought out potential in me that I was not aware I had. It has gotten me into state, getting me up early, getting me ready to go. I used to be the person that said I couldn't wake up early. My productivity is way up. It has also bought me time in my day as I get some much accomplished when I first wake up. It's allowed me to build my coaching business at night. I have loved the Morning Fire Academy. It actually works and made it so easy to follow. I'm excited for my future."

— Angel, El Paso, TX

"What a great system this is. You can incorporate it into your routine as well as things at night to get prepared for the morning. Small basic steps that you can do to turn around your life and to change your thinking as well as habits. They aren't overwhelming, and they allow you to change your attitude and your day."

— Steve, Severna Park, MD

"I own a business and before going into the program, I was very scattered with my business, my approach, and my ideas. I was looking for a repeatable system that I could put into place that would help in my business and personally. The Morning Fire gave me just that, and the great thing is I accomplish more in the morning than most people do all day."

— Charlie, Limerick, PA

About the Author

Jeff Wickersham, founder of Morning Fire Coaching and host of the *Morning Fire for Entrepreneurs* Podcast, leads his clients from battling thoughts that plague them, like "I'm not good enough," "I'm not worthy," or "I will never be successful," to discovering they're good enough, uncovering their worth, and achieving unprecedented levels of success.

Jeff helps his clients show up for themselves every morning, own the day, and develop high-performance habits. As a result, they consistently share that these game-changing habits have helped them increase their energy, focus, and abundance. They even say that through harnessing the power of the Morning Fire routine, they have found more time in each day to enjoy their lives.

A sought-after coach, Jeff is based just outside of Philadelphia, Pennsylvania, where he lives with his wife, Heather, and two sons, Jackson and Carter. He is a huge fan of all Philadelphia sports teams and loves to coach youth sports in his spare time.

If you're looking for your own Morning Fire but don't know where to begin, feel free to book a 30-Minute Motivation Session:
https://calendly.com/themorningfire/motivationcall
As a gift to you for reading this book, your first 30-minute motivation call is 100% FREE.

Defining Moments Book Publishing

If you're like many aspiring authors, you have wanted to write a book for a long time. Maybe you have even started a book, but somehow, as hard as you have tried to make your book a priority, other things keep getting in the way.

Finding the time and confidence to write can be a huge obstacle. Some authors have fears about their ability to write, some wonder whether or not anyone will value what they write, and others worry that no one will buy their book. For many, the challenge is simply making the time to write their book or having the accountability needed to finish it.

Most authors get stuck trying to navigate the technical end of publishing. They get overwhelmed with the logistics of finding an editor, finding a support team, hiring an experienced designer, and figuring out all the technicalities of writing, publishing, marketing, and launching a book.

Others have actually written a book and might have even published it, but they did not find a way to make it profitable.

Defining Moments Press helps aspiring authors, life coaches, healers, business professionals, and other non-fiction or self-help authors get their books published without taking years or investing their life savings.

Authors who are looking for an alternative to self-publishing or signing with a major publishing house will find a comprehensive solution in Defining Moments Press.

Defining Moments Press partners with authors who are looking to share transformative ideas with others throughout the world. They offer full profits to their authors, low-priced author copies, and simple contract terms.

Founded by #1 Bestselling Author Melanie Warner, Defining Moments Press prides itself on bringing readers and authors together to find tools and solutions for everyday challenges from people who have overcome them.

Melanie has over 20 years of experience as a writer, publisher, master life coach, and accomplished entrepreneur. She and her team handle all of the technical aspects of book creation so you can spend more time focusing on growing your business and making an impact.

For more information on how to participate in the next Defining Moments Author Training program, find free educational training, or simply learn more about Warner's innovative approach to self-publishing, email melanie@MyDefiningMoments.com.

Other Books By Defining Moments Press

Defining Moments: Coping With the Loss of a Child
— Melanie Warner

Defining Moments SOS: Stories of Survival
— Melanie Warner and Amber Torres

Write Your Bestselling Book in 8 Weeks or Less and Make a Profit—Even if No One Has Ever Heard of You
— Melanie Warner

Beyond Brilliant: Roadmap From Fear to Courage
— Shiran Cohen

Ravens and Rainbows
— Vanessa Ruda

Life Mapping: Decoding the Blueprint of Your Soul
— Karen Loenser

Printed in Poland
by Amazon Fulfillment
Poland Sp. z o.o., Wrocław

79619641R00060